Pigs eat Wolves

Comments About Pigs Eat Wolves

"Charles Bates lights a fire under an old warning tale for little children, challenging our comfortable perceptions. He shows that the sweet pigs, their well-meaning mother, and the cunning wolf—as well as the objects and settings of the story—contain a complex, psychologically true account of a process we desperately need to understand. Issues of initiation, maturation, and the assimilation of evil addressed in this story crop up on every curve of our planet. Here is a quick, graspable, and illuminating tool for handling the presence of darkness we fear."

Nor Hall, Ph.D.
Author, *The Moon and the Virgin, The Broodmales*

"I was stunned the first time I heard Charles' rendering of the fairy tale. The words still inform my teaching of leadership. I'm convinced that storytelling of this sort is necessary to understand and face our fears as we seek courage to know and act authentically."

Robert Terry, Ph.D.
Director, Reflective Leadership Program
Hubert H. Humphrey Institute of Public Affairs

"*Pigs Eat Wolves* is an intriguing display of the major issue in psychological and spiritual development—the interplay between what is conventionally labeled as good and evil. Bates illustrates the connection between one's thinking or consciousness and action in the path toward self-mastery. This book is a must for those who seek more discernment as leaders or agents of change. It is a great 'think piece' challenging the reader to go beyond a surface understanding of human nature, differences, and the process of change."

Darya Funches, Ph.D.
Chairwoman & CEO, the REAP Gallery Unlimited Corp.
Chairwoman of the Board, NTL Institute for Applied Behavioral Studies

"Bates makes us realize that the unconscious is our ally and its power is available for our use."

Justin O'Brien, Ph.D.
Author, *The Wellness Tree*
Past Director of Education, Marylebone Holistic Health Centre, London

"Charles has written a much-needed treatise on how to come in contact with your dark side and not only come out OK, but grow. Globally we must develop beyond the "us and them" mentality that now dominates: our survival depends on it. Recognizing that all polarities exist in each of us is one essential step in developing the community of humankind. Charles has given us an image and metaphor of how to take that step."

Carolyn Lukensmeyer, Ph.D.
Professional Staff, Gestalt Institute of Cleveland

PIGS EAT WOLVES

GOING INTO PARTNERSHIP WITH YOUR DARK SIDE

Charles Bates

AFTERWORD by ROBERT BLY
ILLUSTRATED by MIKE McCOLL

YES INTERNATIONAL PUBLISHERS
St. Paul, Minnesota

Other books by Charles Bates:

Ransoming the Mind: An Integration of Yoga and Modern Therapy
Mirrors for Men: Affirmations & Actions for Daily Reflection
(with Justin O'Brien)

FIRST YES INTERNATIONAL PAPERBACK EDITION PUBLISHED IN 1991.

Library of Congress Cataloging in Publication Data

Bates, Charles, 1942-
    Pigs eat wolves: going into partnership with your dark side /
Charles Bates; illustrated by Mike McColl.
      p. cm.
    Includes bibliographical references.
    ISBN 0-936663-04-9
    1. Maturation (Psychology) 2. Shadow (Psychoanalysis)
3. Personality and culture. 4. Three little pigs. I. Title.
BF710.B38 1991
155.2'5—dc20   91-12072
                                         CIP

To my teacher,
the wolf in my life.

Acknowledgements

The contributions of my teacher, to whom this book is dedicated, extend far beyond words. He has left me unfettered, and at the same time, has shown me a guiding love out of which I continually draw strength and courage.

I owe a deep debt of gratitude to Louise McCannel, whose generous support has made this book possible. Over the years her gracious patronage of my work—from painting to writing—has eased my way on the creative journey.

I warmly acknowledge the brotherly nurturance of Robert Bly who took time from his own writing to read and reread this manuscript, give me his encouragement and feedback, and write the inspiring last pages of this book.

Many thanks to my esteemed colleague, Charlie Seashore, for his enthusiastic support and his compelling invitation to the readers of these pages.

During the course of my career there have been many, far too numerous to mention, who have contributed to my thinking and personal growth. Special thanks, however, goes to the Gestalt Institute of Cleveland's Organizational and Systems Development staff for modeling their clarity and impeccable thinking process.

My appreciation to the Family Services of Greater St. Paul for creatively assisting in the birth of this book.

For reading the manuscript and offering their invaluable suggestions, I wish to thank Justin O'Brien, Eileen Polinger, and Syl Jones. For their continued support in all my work, I thank Bob Terry, Yvonne Cheek and Archie Givens. Special appreciation to Mike McColl for his brilliant illustrations.

Finally, a special thanks to Theresa, whose questions, criticism, suggestions, and long hours of rewriting with me have been invaluable in making this book what it is.

Introduction

I assume Jung has been paying close attention to recent developments that elaborate and expand some of the key concepts he has sponsored in our quest to understand our human condition. I am sure he is amused to see that not even the Three Little Pigs has escaped our attention in looking for ways to explore the concept of the shadow, or dark side, of our nature. Little did we know when we heard and reheard the telling of this story that each of us turns out to incorporate not only all three of those little pigs but the big bad wolf as well.

The compelling nature of childhood stories and fairy tales is evident again through the power of myth and symbol. Our intrigue is warranted by the power of these stories to excite our consciousness but also to penetrate into a deeper and more primitive level of our being that may escape our awareness.

Pigs Eat Wolves challenges us to accept, as part of our being, those characteristics which we would like to see only in others. We embody the naive and wishful thinking, the dutiful and plodding sense of responsibility taking, the cautious and fearful wondering, and the outrageous and unpredictably violent side of life. To see and accept within ourselves the full range of our humanity is all that is asked by this enlightening, entertaining, shocking, and delightful recasting of this classic tale.

Charles Bates takes a small number of clearly written pages, with delightful and provocative illustrations, to help us see our total self, the light and the dark, and the gradations in between. If you do not want to be disturbed by this challenge, don't risk reading this book. It says it over and over in different ways: we prefer to project onto others those things we find difficult within ourselves. But it is only an illusory sense of peace that comes from pushing away the difficult sides of self.

Empowerment comes from our openness to all aspects of our nature. Denial leads to much pain, in ourselves and others. Accepting the nurturing, loving mother pig in ourselves is as difficult for some of us as it is for others to come to terms with the big bad wolf.

All this book asks is that we give up the illusion that most, if not all, goodness resides within us and most, if not all, evil exists outside us. A powerful message for a small book.

Charlie Seashore, Ph.D.
Past Chairman, National Training Laboratories
Faculty, Fielding Institute, Santa Barbara, CA

Preface

We all grew up on fairy tales, their telling ransomed from parent, teacher or babysitter with promise of quiet or sleep. Our minds then imagined whole new worlds into existence—worlds richly populated with fantastic creatures, heroic feelings, colorful settings.

From fairy tales we learned that good triumphs over evil, purity comes through innocence, cleverness pays, valor is noble, and princes and princesses are always beautiful. Each of these lessons was summoned from our deep unconscious, or profoundly planted there.

Fairytale, myth, and theater have served the human community in conveying teachings, giving meaning, preserving history, and foretelling the future. The storyteller renders fables, legends, and gossip—stories familiar and foreign—to all ears that listen. Remolded by custom and the needs of the time, each tale passes through the voice of the teller, chronicling social evolution and bearing the imprint of each community's need.

Today, more than ever, we need fairy tales. They have value for us both as children and as adults. The child in us listens in wonder and the adult we have become brings mature experience to the reading. In retelling the stories of our childhood, we go back to the ground of our experience, creating the opportunity to look at ourselves in new ways.

The global community searches for its own maturity as it moves round and round life's carousel. Seeking an unexplored depth in the community soul, seeking leaders moved by a call to compassion, justice, and reflection, seeking their own transformation, men and women reach out to grasp the brass ring for the next ride. Fairytales and myth are the music that gives rhythm, meaning, and excitement to the ride; they are the metaphors and poetry of the human psyche.

1

The story of The Three Pigs is just such a metaphor. It is a map, and its analysis provides an insightful look at human nature. The metaphor is much more than a map, however; it is the terrain itself. Metaphor provides a rich learning environment. When used to model the experience of self-discovery, it provides us the opportunity to observe the larger patterns, analyze the intricacies of behavior, and foresee the obstacles we will encounter in that experience.

Along my way, the fable of The Three Little Pigs has provided me with images that help make meaning of my journey. Through the story, I have come to understand that I am the little pigs as I move through the stages of human development they each represent. I also learned that community and culture, like Mother Pig, have raised me on their stories of life and defined who I am while nurturing me. Most of all, I found that I am often eaten by the wolf.

Life has made it clear that if I am to gain any mastery of myself, my lessons are to be found and contacted inside the arenas I avoid. Knowledge continues to demand that I lift mastery out of the open hands of what I fear.

Meeting the most dangerous person in my life, my spiritual teacher, marked the formal beginning of my journey. He was a conscious wolf who pulled me along the path while making it look as if he was chasing me, paradoxically devouring me when he was nurturing me.

This book evolved out of my understanding of what I have learned. By being pressed against the edges of personal boundaries, I have experienced the essential role of paradox in giving dimension, mystery, and richness to life. Paradox demands that I seek and embrace wholes rather than horde parts as I stumble, walk, and run along the path.

The Three Little Pigs shares a motif used by many cultures under a variety of names. The Italians tell the tale of The Three Goslings; the Africans relate The Tiny Pig; in Turkey the story is told of The Three Hares; and from the French we get The Three Pullets. You may be familiar with only the shortened form of its telling, ending with the wolf's defeat at the brick house. This abridged story robs us of the important lessons of the third pig's trials and his resulting

2

maturation. Some modern editions would have us believe that all the pigs survive the wolf, but that portrayal levels the magnificent structure of systematic human development, including failure, and does us all a disservice. *Pigs Eat Wolves* uses the full version of the story because that version provides us with profound insights into ourselves and a vision for a compelling future.

There are many sides of ourselves that we deny. We are frightened or repulsed by them and do not want to admit them into awareness. For ensuring our survival, we develop protective structures to defend against the power in those denied sides. We bury that power in the darkness, called the unconscious, and there we try to keep it safely out of sight. Our culture, too, tells us what is to be ignored, what is not to be done, and what is wrong. We dutifully store these forbidden areas in the darkness as well.

A time comes in our development when we need to take back what we and our culture have put in the darkness because some of what we have buried there is essential for our next steps.

The story of The Three Little Pigs is a story about that taking back. A tale of an ever-maturing truth, it is full of symbols: the mother represents culture; the wolf personifies the darkness; the three pigs typify the levels of development; the events enact moments and methods of integration.

This is a story of the seeker's quest—a venture into the darkness of the unknown. All of the characters, objects, and actions in the story are you. Attend to this story with care, for the story told is your own.

C B

3

Once upon a time there were three little pigs. They lived with their mother in a happy home in the middle of a peaceful glen.

After their breakfast of porridge, mother pig worked in the garden while the little pigs frolicked and played as much as they liked.

At midday the pigs protected themselves from the sun by rolling in the cool mud on the bank of the stream that ran through their yard. Life was happy for the little pigs, and they thought it would always be so.

The Pigs

The three little pigs are just like us as we enter life and begin the route to maturity. We're all naive at the beginning; personal circumstances then intervene to mature us slowly and carefully or else push us roughly into the face of stark reality. The same pattern of human development, however, is shared by us all. We stand at various stages of growth; where we stand defines what we see and determines the way we make sense of our world.

Each pig represents a stage of development common to all of us, yet each pig is also a separate individual, growing to maturity through interaction with others. The pigs will learn that life unfolds in relationship, is tested in relationship, and ultimately matures in relationship. You might find yourself in all three of these pigs, yet one will probably predominate in your life.

The first pig seems frivolous; the second pig wants to do everything just right; the third pig is smart but compulsively defensive. They are all naive, beginning their quests as impotent innocents. Life will serve as a theater for the three pigs to act out each stage of development and outgrow their innocence. When they survive they will be initiated into a new definition of self, empowered with a new maturity; when they don't, they will be consumed by what they continually ignore.

Mother Pig

Mother pig symbolizes the unconscious nurturing source, the psyche, the collective memory of culture, the Universal Mother. The pigs' entire view of life is fed to them through her. Living with mother—a loving power but the only power— is having everything magically taken care of. Though they do not know it, she is their own self, the giver of all life. From her appears all that is needed without any effort on the part of the little pigs. Mother pig embodies culture, showing them how to live their lives, telling them what must be remembered, defining their roles, shaping their beliefs, preserving their stories and music and dance.

Each pig's connection with this source is immature and

mostly unconscious. Their connection does not have the power of an awakened relationship and remains, therefore, naive. In order to make the connection to that source real and potent, the pigs must become aware of, and go beyond, their ties to their mother.

In the evenings after the pigs had eaten supper, mother pig would clean up the kitchen and ready the children for bed. Dressed in pajamas, the little pigs would eagerly gather around their mother in front of the hearth. Then she would tell them stories—stories of the big bad wolf who lived in the nearby forest, stories of caution and warning, stories that often made their little curly tails straighten. Each night she ended her fable with an instruction to be wary of the big bad wolf because he was fond of eating little pigs.

The Wolf

The wolf is the designated evil one. He represents everyone's dark side, the shadow, the individual and collective unacceptable aspects of the pigs' minds. We could say he is the despised self. The wolf is created by the mother's fears and the pigs' naivete. What culture and the pigs cannot and do not claim in themselves becomes the fiber and behavior of the wolf.

Culture forms a wolf by compelling us to develop certain sides of ourselves and deny others. It says to us: "Be a good boy." "Girls don't do that." "Never tell a lie." "Girls are pretty and nice." "Boys don't cry." "Don't touch yourself there." "Do what you are told."

This denial, at times essential for our preservation, leaves much to develop in the darkness of our unconscious mind. All that culture considers good, it relegates to the light of awareness, and all that it considers bad, it ignores and relegates to the darkness. Both are enforced in the name of the protective community. The womb of darkness, holding our forgotten pasts along with our unknown futures, is then maligned by culture because our despised selves and our evil is buried there. Culture blames the darkness for what it hides.

We form our own wolf by ignoring or repressing everything we do not want to see or know. The wolf is our darkness, holding our unacceptable instincts, fears, anger, violence, insecurity, sexuality, and so on. There we hide away thoughts of revenge, jealousy, animal behaviors that are socially inappropriate, thoughts of incest, rage, greed, physical abuse.

An example of repressing unacceptable behavior can be seen in a woman who often complained about a quality she despised in other women. She found weakness in women to be distasteful, manipulative and annoying. Whenever she judged women to be less strong than herself, she saw weakness. Her reaction to this quality was to refuse to take on a "weak" stance herself and to compulsively challenge any woman she encountered using it. By making these women the designated evil ones, however, she did not have to look at her own weakness. She was blind to her own manipulative behavior. The "despised" persons were reflections of her own need to render life

11

harmless, and the wolf she created was formidable.

"From these repressed qualities, which are not admitted or accepted because they are incompatible with those chosen, the shadow is built up."* When this shadow is not accepted or explored, it functions outside of our awareness and our lack of scrutiny allows it added power.

The dark side also holds the collective denials of culture which it projects onto groups, defining them as evil in some way. Because it has displaced its unacceptable drives onto this "outside" group, society can feel safe. Criminals, for example, hold our collective violence; Blacks embody our fear of darkness; American Indians hold the shame and guilt of genocide; homosexuals hold our cultural rejection of same-sex admiration; women hold the anxiety of annihilation by the creative force. These groups are our fears projected as our despised ones. They carry our evil, relieving us of the burden. We are not evil; they are. The pigs are innocent; the wolf is bad. The big, bad wolf may live deep in the dark woods, but he is very much alive and has a significant influence on the pigs.

---

* Marie-Louise Von Franz, *Shadow and Evil in Fairytales*. 1987, Spring, p. 6.

One day while watching her children at play, the wise mother pig knew that at last it was time for her children to go out on their own to seek their fortunes. So with tears in her eyes and final words of caution about the wolf, she sent them off, each on his separate way, to face the world.

Departure

The pigs are about to embark on a new venture. Until now they have lived only one side of life—the side of innocence and light. Now they must enter into a world where both sides of life—light and darkness—co-exist. The pigs' departure will bring them into contact with the unknown, into contact with the darkness they have ignored. Much of their self-definition and personal power was acquired from their mother. They ceded the rest to those forces that function in the darkness outside of their awareness. On their quest the pigs must encounter what has been rendered unacceptable and invisible by culture (mother pig's stories) and their own development. They must become aware of the paradox of life, what Nicholas of Cusa calls the "co-existence of opposites." The pigs' adventure will now take them into the real world but the wolf lives there too.

Joseph Campbell says that departure is an essential step on the hero's journey* and one which is found in the mythology of all cultures. East Indian, Nachiketa, departs from home to confront the God of Death; Australian Aborigines go "walk about"; American Indians embark on a vision quest. The motif of departure often includes being sent off by a parent figure of the opposite sex. The miller's daughter is sent on her encounter with Rumplestiltskin because of her father's bragging; Jack begins his adventure on the beanstalk after being sent to market by his mother; Beauty is sent to the beast by her feckless father; Hiawatha's quest is inspired by the stories of his grandmother, Nokomis; Eve is ordered from the garden into the world by her heavenly Father.

Embarking on a new venture is at once a delicate and a powerful occurrence. As we depart from the safety of the known we embrace the mystery of life's unknowns. The change signals that our ensuing approach to the world will be quite different from the way it was before.

---

* Joseph Campbell. *The Hero with a Thousand Faces.* 1949, Princeton University Press, p. 58.

15

Initiation

We must always step outside the protection of the "garden of Eden" to be initiated into maturity. What we do with what we encounter outside the garden determines our maturation and the level of our initiation. While any act that takes us across a boundary can be an initiation, self unfoldment follows two initiatory paths: gateway initiations and process initiations. The extraordinary events of gateway initiations cause immediate change. Process initiations, on the other hand, bring about transformation through the actions of everyday life. The pigs' departure from mother amounts to a gateway initiation, as was our first day of kindergarten or moving into our first apartment. Process initiations, however, will unfold for the pigs over time as they interact with the wolf, much as we mature with another in the interactions of married life.

In order to achieve a fully mature self, the pigs' shadow dimension must be explored and integrated. Their maturity will evolve with the integration of the opposites of good and evil, light and dark, mother pig and wolf, self and other. This integration brings about an opportunity for a maturity that would have been impossible with one-sided development, whether that side be the mystery of darkness or the knowledge of light.

Integration sometimes necessitates conflict. By being faithful to what we have already learned and encountering what is new, we frequently experience conflict. Leaving home often proves to be a series of conflicts between light and dark, safety and danger, known and unknown. The little pigs, for example, will be in conflict because they are going into the realm of life where the wolf lives, but they were told by their mother to avoid contact with him. In fact, for the pigs' integration, contact with the wolf is essential.

Antagonistic Cooperation

In initiation, opposite forces work together to serve full self-integration. Heinrich Zimmer refers to this work as "antagonistic cooperation," stating that, "every lack of integration in the human sphere simply asks for the appearance, somewhere in space and time, of the missing opposite."* The wolf is called forth to fill that void.

Because the pigs are naive, they create the wolf as despised. Because they are naive, the wolf stands for the side of themselves they reject. For self-mastery, however, the whole self must be embraced. The wolf is the dark part of the pigs' self, and at the same time, he is the gatekeeper at the garden of self-knowledge. In order to gain entrance, the pigs must inevitably pass the wolf who insists that they be impeccable before progressing to the next stages of their development. He stands between the pigs and life—first as a devouring guard, later as a worthy adversary and mentor. The wolf can be viewed in many roles, but he always demands to be recognized!

Lucifer and Prometheus, both dark figures, hold intriguing similarities. Lucifer means "light bearer," and Prometheus brought fire to humanity. Both were punished yet both provided invaluable contributions. A Kabbalist rabbi friend gave me an enlightening interpretation of Lucifer that confirmed these similarities. According to esoteric Jewish tradition, God chose Lucifer to mentor humanity for its eventual rule of heaven. He was the only servant wise enough and devoted enough to adhere strictly to the stewardship of knowledge. Playing the "wolf" for humanity, Lucifer demanded true competence and wisdom from the children of God before they would be allowed to rule heaven.

Another "wolf" is the nemesis, Murphy. His task is the same: to demand excellence. Murphy's First Law states, "If something can go wrong, it will." If we attempt a change before we are capable of managing it, Murphy's "law" will stop us. On one side, Murphy personifies our lack of impeccability; on the other side, Murphy ensures that we not move on until we have the competency to fully embrace the growth experience. Because they point directly to the work we need to do on ourselves in ascending to knowledge, our mistakes are Murphy's gifts to us.

Life and the wolf are intertwined. Because the pigs fear darkness and what lies buried in it, they associate the wolf with

* Heinrich Zimmer. *The King and the Corpse.* 1948, Princeton Bollinger, p. 34, 38.

17

annihilation. When the pigs' logic is the logic of fear, the wolf becomes a source of annihilation and needs to be avoided. When the pigs' logic is the logic of engagement, the wolf becomes a source of growth and needs to be encountered. Contact with the wolf is thus paradoxical: on the one hand dangerous and on the other essential.

The wolf exists for the pigs' learning. Maturity, potency, and command of inner conflict occurs through day-to-day contact with the wolf. In the eternal play of opposites, the wolf is the teacher, but appears so only after the pig develops into a qualified student. Until then, the wolf remains that which devours naive ones. Eventually, we all seem to learn that the wolf can neither be tamed nor destroyed; it must be engaged. Like us, the pigs will have to discover a way to live safely in the world with the wolf.

The first little pig waved goodbye to his mother and dashed away, skipping gaily down the road. By and by he came upon a man carrying a load of straw. "Mr. Man," he said, "will you please give me some straw to build my house?"

The man gave him all he wanted and the little pig set to building his house of straw. He hurried with construction and was soon dancing and playing in the sun again.

The First Pig and His House of Straw

Are you surprised that the man gave the little pig building materials without requiring any exchange? In one sense, the straw and all it symbolizes are qualities that already belonged to the pig, resources inherited through his mother. From prenatal symbiosis to the wisdom of old age, each pig possesses the raw potentials to expand or build anew the lodging of his awareness. In itself, potential is impotent until made actual, and therefore potent, through awareness and use. The straw used by the first little pig can be viewed as base potential made into a useable structure.

The first little pig knows only how to be aware of what is temporary and flimsy. Because his awareness is limited and unsophisticated, flimsy substances are all he can request. He can build only with what he has already claimed; his house is the symbol of himself. We may even say that the little pig builds his new life with straw.

Although a coarse, base substance, the grossest of the grasses, straw proves insubstantial to stand up to the intensities of life. The flimsiness of straw corresponds to the pig's whimsical nature. He is a child—naive, mostly unconscious, easily impressionable, and ignorant of his connection to life. The little pig acts just like a wide-eyed farm boy coming to the big city for the first time, a huckster's delight. His innocence makes him an easy victim and vulnerable prey for the wolf.

First Pig Thinkers

When we naively do everything we are told, thinking we are being good, we exhibit first-pig thinking. Some of us use this thinking all our lives, often finding ourselves in abusive relationships, personal or professional. First-pig thinkers do not have the ability to say no, nor can they establish strong boundaries. Because their ego remains underdeveloped and flimsy, they are easily trespassed by the will of others. Like magnets, they seem to draw abusive people to themselves. In a child, innocence charms and evokes protection, but in an adult it can become tedious, eliciting possible misuse.

One first-pig thinker, a naive and retiring woman, avoided

serious or in-depth conversations with men. As a child she was taught to do whatever men told her. Her weak boundaries left her unprotected and compelled her to obey once a man made any advance in her direction. In defense she kept all her conversations with men light, frivolous, and superficial, never allowing them close enough to obligate her or make her a victim of their "authority." Consequently her needs were unmet and her opinions were never expressed. She waited for them to be magically fulfilled and understood. The tragedy of this behavior left her alone, locking out satisfying adult relationships and thoroughly hiding her wolf.

Let us return to the story to see how the first pig fared.

After a short time, who should appear on the road but the big, bad wolf. Seeing the little pig, he began to drool, and without a thought, rushed forward to eat him up. The little pig scurried into his house of straw squealing with terror, just managing to slam the door in the wolf's face.

Very angry, the wolf growled, "Little pig, little pig, let me come in!"

The pig feebly replied, "No, no, no! Not by the hair of my chinny, chin chin!"

"Well, then," said the wolf mockingly, "I'll huff, and I'll puff, and I'll blow your house in."

So the wolf inhaled deeply, his massive chest expanding like a bellows, and he huffed and he puffed and he easily blew the house in. Then in a flash he greedily ate the little pig up, squeal and all.

So much for naivete! Ignorance of the darkness is no match for its power. The little pig thought he was ready for life, but he was aware of only a very narrow range of resources. By not analyzing and contemplating the stories he swallowed whole at his mother's knee, he lived an unexamined life. The strength he possessed was not his strength; the right answers he professed were not his answers. The resulting lack of protection and self-knowledge did not prepare him for life's intensity. He knew how to be protected and taken care of, but he did not know how to protect and take care of himself. Like his house, the structure of his ego was very weak and made him incapable of standing up to life. Ignorance made him vulnerable and consumed him.

In fairy tales, the motif of purity through innocence is a common theme. Instances of purity defined as youth and freedom from worldly knowledge typically win the kingdom. This time we find a twist. In this story, entrance to the kingdom demands purity acquired through maturity.

Personal development occurs in stages. We learn how to be competent on one level of development before moving on to the next. The first level serves as foundation for the second level, the second for the third, and so on.

As we have seen, the first pig stage corresponds to the beginner's level of development. It is that part of us that knows only how to recognize and sustain simple contact with reality. The first pig, satisfied with what is already within him, frivolously refuses to learn anything new. Believing his strength is at its peak, he thinks he knows it all. Intellectually lazy, he acts on the first information he receives, looking no further. This ignorance makes him culpable, binding him inside limited thinking.

First pig thinkers also refuse to change, to examine or think for themselves. They refuse to chew solid food because pre-digested mother's milk is always there. First pig thinking narcissistically centers on the first pig. It does not notice the impact its behavior has on the larger environment.

First pig thinking is focusing on "me" and "mine" and not being aware of "us."

It is refusing to change our habits, even when others tell us they are hurtful.

It is selling our virgin forests for short term profit.

It is sending jobs abroad to reduce costs, while undoing the fabric of our labor force.

It is insisting that our belief is the only one, ignoring the larger world community.

It is stubbornly believing that where we are now is the only truth.

We may say that first pig thinking is seductive; it can be used as an excuse to avoid change. Because they live blithely inside their unexamined notions, first pig thinkers can feel "good"—justified and righteous—while ignoring the wider implications of a "good" life.

"Good" people are consumed by their wolves all the time and they don't even know they are being consumed. Some of them even make a virtue out of being devoured. Inside the belief systems acquired in childhood, they presume themselves right. Actually they may be supporting "isms" like racism, sexism, and narrow nationalism by not carefully examining those beliefs and attendant behavior. By projecting their dark sides onto their designated evil ones, they rob themselves of the opportunity to grow and to recognize the pain they inflict. First pig thinkers do not even realize the impact they have on others.

An incident I witnessed will illustrate this point. Last Christmas a twenty-three-year-old man had what he thought was a good idea. He was "inspired" to give the family dog away to a troubled boy in need of a pet. So without consulting anyone in his family, the man put a bow on the dog's collar and brought it to its new home. The probable pain to his brother and sister was invisible to him and the awful possibility of having to take the gift back did not occur to him. All he could see was the immediate idea of the boy needing something to love. When the repercussions of horror rippled through his family, he could not understand what all the fuss was about. He had a good idea, he did it.

The Tyranny of Weakness

The flimsiness of the first pig thinker's boundaries unsettles others; its weakness can be tyranny. In groups, people tend to adjust their behavior to the feeblest member while the vital feelings and behaviors of the other members often go unexpressed. Another man, for example, grew up in a family tyrannized by a "weak" father. No one could express excitement or voice a disagreement because they might upset father, causing him to have a heart attack. Many people walk around on proverbial egg shells because they are manipulated by someone else's expressed inability to cope with truth. This unstable ego structure characterizes first pig behavior—manipulative, self-centered, often tyrannical.

Stuck in their narrowness, first pig thinkers are not able or willing to be aware of others. Somewhat acceptable in a child, selfishness proves oppressive in an adult. First pig thinkers unfortunately exclude themselves from life by putting others in the position of deciding what truths, and therefore what parts of life, they can bear. Those close to the weak tyrant may create a habit of withholding sides of themselves deemed too intense. Partners and family of a first pig thinker often become compulsive withholders, eventually withholding even from themselves.

Not surprisingly, the exclusiveness of self-indulgent weakness causes the first pig's downfall. Focus on "me" has value, but breaks down quickly when it is the only choice used, symbolized by the wolf blowing down the house of straw.

Expanding Awareness

How many times have we all come to a gateway in our lives only to be eaten by the wolf? We find ourselves frustrated and discouraged, cycling again and again to the same impasse. The question is, can we ever progress beyond first pig thinking and our ideas of straw? Yes, we can, because our awareness grows with time.

Years ago, my family took a vacation to Banff National Forest in Canada. Hiking up a mountain path, we spotted wild raspberries growing in the underbrush. My nine-year-old son could not see them.

27

Although we all pointed the berries out to him, we were amazed that he still could not spot them. All the way up the mountain, we picked berries to share with him, joking that we would refuse to feed him on the way down. In frustration, my son foraged carefully in the bushes until he learned to spot the raspberries for himself. Through mouthfuls of berries, he voiced his surprise that he had been missing them. On the way down, the rest of us suddenly discovered strawberries growing along the path exactly where we had been picking raspberries on the way up. Why hadn't we seen them before? We realized that we shared the same lack of awareness as my son. Now, with our expanded awareness, we could all enjoy strawberries as well as raspberries, except for my son, of course, who couldn't see the strawberries at all!

In life, each of us can see only what we know how to see. Everything is always right in front of us, but our experience occurs inside our awareness. For all of us, awareness grows with time. Life manifests in change and growth with various levels of experience present inside the same event. This is quite evident when we remember how a mature adult and a child see the same situation.

Let's return to our story and see what the second little pig does with the same situation.

The second pig left his mother determined to follow her advice and do well. Walking cautiously down the road, he came upon a man carrying a large bundle of sticks. He said to the man, "Mr. Man, will you please give me some sticks to build my house?"

The man gave him all he wanted and the little pig set to building his house of sticks. Construction took the pig a bit longer than it took his brother, but after careful work, the house of sticks was completed. Feeling he had done the right thing, he ran outside to play.

The Second Pig

The second little pig always tries to do the right thing. He wants to please others and seeks appropriate behavior to that end, yet his inadequate ideas about life render him confused, tentative, and rigid. Smarter than his brother, he attempts to make a stronger structure to shelter himself. Although conscious that there is something he needs to do, he does not know how to know what it is. Like his brother, he builds his house with the limited resources he has available—sticks, a logical extension of straw. The little pig recognizes how different sticks are from straw, but he cannot realize how much they are the same.

Sometimes whole communities can be second pigs. Recently two ethnic groups were locked in conflict, adding to years of deep-rooted and historical tension. The larger community had political and economic control of the city and traditionally excluded the other group from any decision making. In the ceremonies on Founder's Day, the minority group was seriously slighted. There were hurt feelings and mounting antagonism from the minority. The powerful group decided to make amends by an act of charity to the minority community. When their attempt at atonement provoked even more anger, the group in power was befuddled. They wondered what they had done wrong, and in not understanding, became angry themselves.

We can say that the majority community members were trapped in second-pig thinking. They did not even know how to know what they did wrong. In trying to do the right thing and correct the earlier injustice, they used the same thinking that had caused it. When they should have invited the wounded parties to help plan the menu, they offered a bone of appeasement. Because the majority had made both decisions on its own, its act of atonement was only an extension of the same exclusive thinking that had created the schism. They knew that slighting and appeasement were different; they did not see that both were acts of arrogance.

At the setting of the evening sun, the big bad wolf spied the second little pig and confidently approached the house of sticks. Seeing the wolf coming, the pig scurried inside his house, barred the door, and quaked in anticipation.

The wolf knocked heavily and in a booming voice said, "Little pig, little pig, let me come in."

"No, no, no! Not by the hair of my chinny chin chin," said the little pig shakily.

The impatient wolf threw back the reply, "Then I'll huff, and I'll puff, and I'll blow your house in."

So the wolf blew himself up even bigger than before. And he huffed and he puffed and he puffed and he huffed and he blew the house in. He immediately ate up the astonished little pig, including his squeal.

The Second Pig and the House of Sticks

In the end, the second pig fared no better than his brother. The sticks, while stronger, yielded little more protection than the straw. His shift from straw to sticks was an attempt to accommodate change by merely doing more of the same. The method of the first pig was one-step thinking; the method of the second pig is one-pattern thinking. The second pig choicelessly bound himself by the linear sequence of events that went before. He had not yet matured to the point where he could see larger connections and prevent himself from being consumed. Extending the norm was his only strategy for change. This inadequate problem-solving strategy has the effect of rearranging the furniture when an entirely new structure is needed. Needless to say, the pig was doomed to fail. He forgot the French proverb, "The more things change, the more they remain the same."

In the period immediately following a divorce people often use this method of extending the norm. They almost invariably find a new mate who actually embodies the same characteristics as their old mate. The new relationship, however, will bring up the same conflicts, or will show clear signs of being fitted into the mold of past unexamined behavior because, in fact, both parties bring their wolves with them.

Second Pig Thinking

Second-pig thinking is trying to do the right thing by employing the same principles that have proven themselves inadequate. Taking a logical next step out of a set of beliefs that no longer serves is confusing and frustrating.

We can see this pattern with a woman who spent several years trying to heal a painful relationship with her husband by using the "right answers" supplied by culture. She had already outgrown the boundaries set for women by society, but was not aware of it. Thus she could only keep trying the same remedy again and again. She attempted to guess what her husband was thinking, she tried to change her character, her behavior, the environment. The woman turned herself inside out trying to understand why her solutions were not working. Confused and frustrated, she kept trying to improve herself inside the imbedded expectations of culture's traditional norms for marriage. It didn't occur to her that this realm of inquiry was the main stumbling block. It could only yield the same dysfunctional results she had found so disastrous to her relationship until now.

This woman resembles the second pig in her use of "more" as a strategy for transformation. The second pig built on the past experience of the first pig and came up with a sound, logical answer to the problem of the wolf: use sticks, stronger vegetation. In the face of the wolf, however, building with sticks, an extension of straw, proved to be nothing but an extension of the same frivolous thinking. An old saying applies here: "If you always do what you've always done, you'll always get what you've always gotten." The pig employed the logical extension of old behavior and got the same outcome: he got eaten. Whenever we, like the pig, attempt to use outmoded behavior, the wolf will eat us up.

There was once a man who circled from his therapist, to his support group, to his spiritual director, and back again to his therapist seeking advice. He ran around trying to do the "right" thing, getting confused because there were so many "right" things, some of which did not feel "right" at all. He was unable to see that he had outgrown some of his values, and because of this, life became difficult for him to track in the old way. Attempting to fit his profoundly maturing life inside of a now-inadequate value system, he became frustrated and depressed. Since he used old guides for his behavior, he found himself consistently traveling down dead ends. Similar to the second pig's struggle, the man's struggle involved the awareness that values, like ideas, have careers, and upon periodic examination, some values will naturally be retired for more mature ones. When he was able to realize this, the confusion ended.

Taking Responsibility

Another aspect of second-pig thinking is the notion that circumstances control one's life. This makes life for second-pig thinkers rather obscure. They are apt to think that one thing after another happens to them, when actually they do the same thing over and over. In missing this point, they attempt to engage the wolf in ways that prevent their survival.

Like the house of sticks in which they live, second pig thinkers are locked into a rigid, but weak, system. They feel powerless to give direction to their own lives; things just seem to happen to them. They have a rather brittle idea about how life should be, most often having nothing to do with how it really is. If only others (the wolf) would stop doing things to them, life would improve.

I used to be under the impression that other people were responsible for my emotions. When I was angry, I was sure that someone made me angry, and I could relate in detail how that was so. I likewise thought that people made me fall in love, made me sad, gave me hope, and so on. Of course, people contributed to all these experiences, but did they cause my experience? To the extent that I blamed others for my responses, I was eaten by the wolf. There was no way, however, that anyone could have convinced me of this fact. At some point, I became aware that I had many more choices that I realized and I gave myself permission to use them. In an "angry" encounter, I became aware that I could shout, cry, dissuade, ignore, laugh, or leave the room. I realized that I chose my emotions and was the major creative force in my life.

The second pig thinker is the victim who has the power to change, but lacks the awareness or the courage to do it. Like the majority of us, he thinks having less power is having no power and thus stays bound to old dysfunctional patterns. The Charles Schultz comic strip artfully portrays second pig thinking in its characterization of Charlie Brown. Charlie tries to kick a football held for him by his nemesis, Lucy. She inevitably jerks the football away at the last moment, causing him to crash unceremoniously to the ground. Lucy continually promises not to do it again, but she does it without fail. Every Charlie Brown has his Lucy; he creates her at every moment. Will he ever learn that she will always pull the football away whenever he tries to kick it? Until he does something different, his house of sticks will continue to be blown in and he, too, will be eaten up.

Conscious Incompetence

When a major structure does not work for us any more, the process of life (as well as our own sanity) demands that we stay at it until we discover why it failed. In that light, the failure of the second pig is an important dimension of growth. It points the way from conscious incompetence to conscious competence. The second pig showed us conscious incompetence—things did not work for him and he did not know why. But once we've experienced that for awhile, we can move on to conscious competence—understanding why things work and making efforts to keep it so. Conscious incompetence provides an essential ingredient for human and spiritual development, keeping us pressed up against our developmental edge in the midst of failure until we realize why we fail.

For millennia mystics have recognized and used this natural occurrence with their students. Students are kept standing on the cutting edge of growth until they become aware of those behaviors that no longer satisfactorily serve them. The teachers ensure that they remain in this state of creative incompetence until they realize the truth.

A friend of mine, a dynamic natural leader, was consistently unable to achieve leadership positions when he joined groups. He would advance to the position of second best, and then at some point in the process, be viewed as a threat to the organization and inevitably be walled out. In his late forties he came to understand that his "incompetence" to be number one was, in some way, his own choice. Indeed, in his youth he did not behave as a leader, even though he had potential, and as he matured into competency over the years, he did not behave any differently. He did not know how to assert his competence. The man was unaware of the depth of his habit of being second best which blocked any insight to his childhood feelings of inadequacy and shame buried deep in his shadow. With just a little effort his wolf was able to blow in his unexamined house of sticks. A wise mentor intervened, keeping him pressed against the boundary of leadership and group inclusion until he was able to work through many layers of shadow to insight and new behavior.

Moving beyond second pig thinking requires an expansion of contact with life; growth into more mature behavior is imperative. Until then, second pig thinkers will live a life of developmental drift, unaware of what works for them, and what doesn't. Until then life will confuse and consume them. Until then they are unable to engage the wolf and survive. Until then their lack of maturity locks out essential awareness for satisfactory contact with life. Until then they get eaten every time.

The third little pig was sad when he left home, as is often true in partings. Walking down the road, he met a man with a hod of bricks. He said to the man, "Mr. Man, will you please give me some bricks to build my house?"

The man gave him all he wanted and the little pig set to building his house of bricks. It was a long and difficult task and he completed it with a deep sense of satisfaction. Then he went outside to plant his garden.

The Third Pig

The third pig was secure and prepared for going into the world. He had pondered deeply the stories told by his mother; he assimilated them and made them his own. His self-assurance was born from this bonding, allowing him to make the developmental shifts necessary for his adventure. Inner confidence gave him the courage to examine himself and extended into the creation of a safe dwelling—a house of bricks. As if pigs were habituated to being devoured, the first two pigs had compulsively repeated their unexamined behavior and were eaten by the wolf. The brothers made decisions based on conditioning, much like someone steering a motorboat by looking back at the wake, eventually circling around into the same errors (and into the wolf's mouth) every time.

Stepping beyond the decisions of the first two pigs in a radically different fashion, the third pig made a move of genius: he used bricks. The logical extension of straw is sticks; the logical extension of sticks is logs. But in realizing that the extension is merely more of the same thing, the third pig made a radical shift of thinking. This reminds me of a favorite comedy group which, when unable to make a transition from one skit to the next, sends someone on stage to announce: "And now for something completely different." Like this proclamation, the third pig tried something completely different from anything pigs had tried before.

One warm summer afternoon, a group of friends spilled out onto the front porch to enjoy a whisper of breeze and tall glasses of sun tea. A disagreement started between their host and hostess and soon escalated into an argument. As if animated by an invisible force, they each got locked into intractable defensive positions, made more difficult by the presence of their friends. The husband was losing ground and beginning to sound as if he was more interested in winning than in getting to the bottom of the conflict, when suddenly he turned on his heel and stomped into the house. In the awkward hush that followed, a few weak jokes were tried to melt the tension. Shortly the door opened again and the husband emerged wearing all his clothes inside out and backwards.

While inside the house, the husband realized that his defenses were working against him, cutting off his ability to communicate. He felt that everything was inside out and backwards, so he decided to dress the part. His strange appearance at the door was so unlike his usual self that it radically changed the atmosphere on the porch. The shift brought delight to the guests and allowed the couple to resolve their difference almost instantaneously. Their usual argument followed an established formula of dysfunctional interaction, unconscious agreement requiring them to act out the whole sad script. This time the husband interrupted the pattern by doing something completely different. The shift brought a totally new and unknown solution into existence. They could now choose.

The House of Bricks

When the third pig chooses something different to build with, he likewise opens· the possibility for a different outcome. For his building material he taps the underlying source, the substance of the unconscious, symbolized by the earth. The shift from sticks to the substance of earth is a shift of genius. He makes a structure based on his acquired knowledge and self-examination rather than personal or cultural habit. He uses the knowledge of the first two levels of awareness but is no longer bound by their limitations. By creating something that didn't exist before from fired clay—the mixture of earth, water, and fire—the pig consciously creates his own experience of life. He is now solidly prepared for the future dimensions of his quest: facing the wolf.

Some time later, the big bad wolf spied the little pig working outside his home. He walked boldly up to the gate. The little pig saw him coming and ran quickly into his house, bolting the door.

The wolf was quite confident in getting what he wanted because he had been so successful with the other pigs. So he knocked arrogantly on the door saying, "Little pig, little pig, let me come in." The little pig haltingly answered, "No, no, no! Not by the hair of my chinny chin chin."

The wolf smirked, "Right. That's what your brothers said, and I ate them up. If you don't open the door, I'll huff and I'll puff, and I'll blow your house in."

He blew himself up so big that the buttons popped right off his shirt. He released a gale of wind against the door. He huffed and he puffed, and he puffed and he huffed, and he huffed and he puffed again. All to no avail. The brick house stood steady against his assault. The astounded wolf lay spent at the door, temporarily defeated.

Defences

At last a pig who can stand up to the wolf! The ingenuity of his decision to try something different has paid off. The assault of the wolf was formidable, as it often is in life, but the pig survived. He saved his squeal!

Though frightened, the third pig remains safe inside his house. Its bricks and mortar represent the evolutionary learning of species and myth, of institutional and individual preservation, claimed as his own. Now he can live within those walls, a sanctuary against the wolf. In another sense, moving into the brick house represents the change from adolescence to adulthood. For most of us, adult interactions provide a much more empowered (and thus safe) environment than the vulnerable stages of adolescence.

The third pig has created a structure in which he sustains himself in the face of the wolf's onslaught. Because he can have continued and sustained contact with the wolf, a whole new dimension of learning will take place. The first two pigs could not survive with the wolf. They locked themselves out of this opportunity because they were consumed at the beginning of each encounter; their naivete was their defeat.

When my daughter was an adolescent, she was intimidated by an elite clique that formed in her school. Her feelings of intimidation interfered with her school work and her social life. So upset was she that she even threatened to quit school. That weekend her favorite uncle came to visit, spending considerable time with her and providing a new perspective on her worth. By Monday morning she was able to create a defense to help herself: she decided that she didn't care what the clique thought of her; she didn't need them. Thus fortified against the power wielded by the group, she was able to excel again in the larger school community.

The shift from being the victim to having defenses against victimization is the initiation symbolized by the brick house. In building it, the third pig has passed through a gateway to a new beginning. He now has some way to withstand the often confusing, and at times overwhelming, complexities of life represented by the assault of the wolf.

We are like the third pig in that defenses are important in our development. They are necessary because they sustain us and give us a sense of security and self-esteem in the face of life's more over-whelming experiences. The pig's initiation allowed him to make himself safe against the wolf, albeit temporarily. The brick house of defenses is critical for the pig because it will allow him continued awareness of the wolf, staying in contact with everything the wolf represents.

One victory against the dark side cannot yield maturity, however. The wolf will return, as, most assuredly, he must.

Now the wolf, we must understand, is very wise. He has spent a lifetime demolishing houses and devouring the pigs inside. Having learned from all of these experiences, he concluded that it was useless to attempt to penetrate the third pig's fortress directly. So he went away to think about new tactics.

Some time later he returned to the brick house, knocked at the door, and in a very friendly manner addressed the third pig again, "Little pig, this struggle between us is senseless. Come with me to Farmer Brown's turnip patch tomorrow morning. We will both be able to dig as many turnips as we like. Then we can have a feast together."

The pig thought for a moment. Then he answered the wolf saying, "That is a splendid idea. What time shall we meet?"

The wolf replied, "Six o'clock" and departed confident that his plan to trick the pig would unfold smoothly.

The little pig, not trusting the wolf, went at five o'clock. When the wolf came to collect him promptly at six, the pig laughed at the befuddled wolf through the bolted door and said, "I went at five this morning and dug a bunch of big, sweet turnips. They are cooking on the hearth at this very moment."

The wolf was furious, but being experienced in the art of deceiving and eating pigs, he was confident that eventually he would have his way.

Security vs. Imprisonment

The pig has tricked the wolf! He has taken another significant step. He's becoming smart—not wise, mind you, but smart. The wolf has behaviors that he uses to be successful; the pig now claims some of them for himself. In order to do this, he must have close contact with the wolf, which leads to another critical point for him.

While sheltered naively behind the underdeveloped truths of his defenses, the pig presumed himself to be able to master life on his own terms. A temporary sense of victory led him to believe his security made him impervious to the wiles of the wolf. Now he discovers that he must step outside his brick house in order to engage life and enjoy its fruits. There is virtually no precedent in the pig's life for what he must do: move from the safe, defended existence of the brick house into the dangerous specter of the wolf. He must take another look at his safety. For now he sits inside the sanctuary of his own making, comfortable, secure, yet ultimately lonely.

In the early 70's the residents at a drug treatment center for adolescents were directed to act out the story of the three pigs. The third pig represented someone who had successfully gone through treatment and participated in an aftercare program; the wolf represented one dimension of the dark side—the desire to get "high." The wolf continually attempted to seduce the third pig to come out of his house and use alcohol and drugs. The third pig refused. In the debriefing after the drama, the young woman who played the third pig reported that it was boring in the house. She said she felt safe there, but knew that life, fun, and growth was out where the wolf was.

The pig, like us, has to operate from safety in order to survive long enough to learn. If not, the same fate will fall his lot as befell his brothers. He will be eaten. The pig will never discover himself, however, in the safety of the brick house. In order to grow, we all require others in our life. Through others we see who we are. We must make ourselves available to be touched deeply. This happens only in relationship. Cutting ourselves off from relationships will cut us off from life.

51

A woman who had been sexually abused built very strong defenses against men. She decided to have nothing to do with them and resolved to trust none of them. In order to experience safety, her defenses were well advised and served her, but eventually she blamed the people who hurt her for her lack of trust and absence of friendship. After some years she realized that she herself had built her brick house and remained locked inside. From this insight, she became strong enough to think about opening the door and venturing out.

The walls of defense are designed to control life and render it harmless. Through his success in building them, the pig realized his power. There is a certain arrogance here, born out of the fresh experience of power. The pig prematurely thinks he has life all figured out. He is the architect that designed the defenses to keep the wolf out and he is the guard that protects his vulnerability against harm. Later the pig comes to realize that he is imprisoned inside the brick walls. Later still, he realizes that he himself is the warden as well as the prisoner.

Like us, the pig initially blames the wolf for his imprisonment, only eventually realizing that he alone is responsible for being locked in the house. He comes to understand that he has grasped merely a part of truth. By acknowledging his role in creating his limitations, however, the pig lays claim to his dilemma; that key interrupts the pattern of his victimization.

Life knocks repeatedly at our door before we realize that we must step beyond the brick walls of our defenses to engage it with awareness, courage, and cunning.

Departure from the brick house signals a monumental step in the pig's development. Much like his first interruption of pattern (leaving the safety of the mother's home) the third pig now interrupts the fixed patterns of culture and his own experience. He does this by embracing paradox: danger as well as safety.

Paradox

For the pig, paradox will now become a practical reality. Previously he thought one side of life true and the other side false.

Now he becomes aware that the other side possesses the next truths necessary for his development. Sitting, unmoving, at one end of any polarity leaves one lonely and disempowered, as if cut off by blinders. There is no power at either of the poles without awareness of the other.

The pig has to claim the power of the entire continuum that the poles define. He will do this by dialoguing with the wolf as his ideological opposite. Through their "antagonistic cooperation," the pig will step outside his house, pass the point of no return, and begin his engagement with the wolf between the poles. In doing so, he will gain the perspective of both polarities and emerge with the power of each.

Our first inkling of this new thinking occurs when the pig agrees to go to the turnip patch with the wolf at six o'clock but actually goes at five. This behavior lies outside the realm of appropriate pig behavior. In choosing to engage the wolf, however, the pig understands that survival requires the use of dimensions contrary to the one side he habitually uses. At this point he begins to seek truth rather than parroting "right" answers.

Another important initiation for the pig has just taken place. After demonstrating his commitment to the values of culture and self-preservation, he now asks, "What am I protecting? At what price do I protect? Is this bringing me happiness?" He becomes reflective and self-correcting by choosing to reassesses his behavioral and moral precepts. Aware of having tenets that continue to serve him well, he knows that if he holds them exclusively he will be disempowered. His two brothers were choiceless and were eaten by the wolf because they did not examine their values.

Slowly the pig realizes that he and the wolf are inextricably linked. Their strong attraction comes from a bond deep in their psyches. The closer the pig gets to integration, the stronger the attraction to the wolf becomes; the stronger the attraction, the more the wolf reflects the pig's deeper self. One way to know when we are working with our dark side is that we just can't stay away from it, it has our whole attention. We are either very attracted to it, or very repulsed by it. Both result in the same outcome—choicelessness.

A woman was raised in a very innocent, upper class, demure

fashion. She found herself madly attracted to leather-clad "bikers" who were the antithesis of her upbringing. Whenever she was in a state of low self-esteem, she was compelled to seek them out. Her attraction was fueled in part by her need to shock her mother, that is, reject her value system. It also represented the unlived portion of her psyche, that which was exciting, dynamic, forbidden. She was alternately attracted to and repulsed by both sides of her life, and because she did not examine either, she was choiceless in both.

Life is too powerful for one to go forth in blind innocence as did the first pig, and too complex to stay the same as did the second pig. Doing something new, the third pig transcended the security of the brick house, responded to the call to action, and, as a qualified learner, engaged the wolf. Now the pig begins to realize the cooperative nature of the wolf's relationship with him: the wolf is here for the pig's learning.

The Turnip Patch

Going to the turnip patch significantly changes the pig because here he begins to claim his power. Here the teachings about the other side of the paradox present themselves to him. The pig now elects to look at parts of himself that he and his culture have chosen to toss away or not acknowledge. In the turnip patch the pig mines the darkness, sorting through the hidden booty for any gold that might have gotten naively or defensively tossed in it. In this sense the turnip patch event represents the examination of self and the collective. It involves digging up what self (ego) and the collective (culture) bury in the darkness as forbidden and unacceptable.

This examination can happen only when the pig has the courage to challenge the idea that he already has the right answers. Prescribed right answers always have a flavor of, "Whatever is permitted is mandatory and whatever is not permitted is forbidden." Prescribed right answers ensure that behavior is mandated and examination circumvented. They allow no choices.

The pig has now gained access to his shadow by mining the unexamined sides of himself, symbolized by digging up the turnips.

In this way he multiplies his choices and expands his power. This exercise is called "mining for gold."

Within the pig, as within us, lie many behaviors that are base, untrustworthy, unrepresentative, and unacceptable. Some of them should remain buried. Other behaviors, however, if guided by the strong hand of positive intent and ethical behavior, will prove to become a power rather than an obstacle.

Mining For Gold

A bright, young man recently graduated with a degree in law. He wanted to be a good lawyer but was troubled because he assumed he lacked the necessary aggression. Through counseling, he discovered that he had strong negative feelings about the "macho" image. Throughout his college career, he disapproved of his male colleagues' attitudes and behaviors towards women. As a result, he dismissed virtually the entire range of assertive behavior as unacceptable.

Realizing that he was disempowering himself, he was asked to list all the assertive behaviors that he would sometimes do, and second, all the assertive behaviors that he would never do. This second list represented a dimension of his shadow. Now he was in a dilemma: he identified with one side, but clearly realized the value of some things on the other side. His next task was to examine the list of what he would never do and choose some he might use on an experimental basis. These he was asked to put in an "I will do temporarily as an experiment" category. He went off eager to make his discoveries.

After some time, the young man reported that he found he could remain true to his values of respect and human dignity while simultaneously being empowered by a fuller range of human behavior. He did what the pig did at the turnip patch: he embraced the darkness, thus laying claim to a larger share of the continuum. Through courage, careful reassessment, and a growing wisdom, he found ethical power and much needed resources in that which had been buried in the darkness. To identify exclusively with "non-macho" behavior would have caused the whole structure of his success in law to echo hollowly between the walls of mistaken defenses. He would have unnecessarily tossed away behavior that had nothing to do with male dominance. In his second-pig stage, he had rigidly identified with the unexamined "right" behavior of his peers and was continually in danger of being eaten by the wolf through inauthentic behavior toward women. Later he graduated to being safely imprisoned within his brick house of "non-macho" behavior, but he was troubled and disempowered. After his experiment he gained greater access to the whole rather than an exclusive identification with a part.

Because the mining for gold exercise has such potential for powerful change, I'll elaborate the exercise. It has two essential ingredients: a stated want, and a resistance to that want. Think of one intractable problem in your life. Make a list of behaviors around that problem that are acceptable to you. Make another list of behaviors around that problem that are unacceptable to you (things you would not do). From this second list, make a third list called What I Would Do Temporarily As An Experiment. Next, choose one item from this last list around which you will conduct your experiment. This identifies your want. Reflect on the resistances to your want such as embarrassment, fear, a feeling of lack of authenticity, social pressure, etc. Purposefully find a way to bring your want into your everyday experience and notice the resistance and anxiety arising in you as a result. Finally, take note of any benefit that this new behavior might offer you. Assess the benefit, and if you feel more empowered ethically, a deeper sense of connection to yourself, and more power, choose to make the behavior part of your life.

Another man used this exercise to great benefit. He wrestled with a problem of being too good. It made him fearful of ever hurting anyone with his behavior. Goodness worked to his detriment because he never allowed himself to appear "not good." His Acceptable list included: compassion, gentleness, love, service, being understanding, accepting others' bad behavior without complaint. His Unacceptable list included: narcissism, bullying, physical violence, inducing fear in others, lying, verbal put-downs of others, demanding good service for himself. His Experiment list included these two: narcissism and being demanding. The one thing he chose to experiment with was narcissism. It soon became apparent that what he wanted was to live his life for himself rather than solely for others. The resistance came in the form of social pressure from people who wanted him to remain the same. He brought narcissism into his everyday life by doing what he wanted, saying what was on his mind, and letting other people think whatever they wanted to think about his behavior. In noting his anxiety, he realized that his ethics were so strongly skewed toward the good that this new behavior still did not violate the integrity of others. He benefitted from the experiment by gaining the ability to set a direction in his life and to stick to it, regardless of others' agendas for him. He did not choose narcissism; he chose the bits of gold hidden in it.

Trickery

Let us go back to the trickery of the pig. After carefully examining the old order, he is about to establish the new. To ensure this outcome, he steps beyond childhood innocence and tricks the wolf. The use of trickery is actually an ancient method in transformation.

In the Biblical story of Jacob and his mother, Rebecca, trickery is used to gain the father's blessing for Jacob though it belongs by law to his brother, Esau. Jacob and Rebecca are successful in their plan, and by their conspiracy, interrupt a centuries-old pattern. As a result of the shift of power through the father's blessing, Jacob's lineage produced the House of David which was the ancestry of Jesus, the Christ. Like Jacob and Rebecca, the pig resorted to trickery in order to enter safely into the realm inhabited by the wolf.

As we gain awareness and power by mining the darkness, we must be able to discriminate between that which is useful from that which is not useful. It's important to remember the lessons of the first two pigs. If we aren't choiceful about our experiments, or don't examine our choices, we will only trade one blindness for another and be eaten by the wolf. At the same time, the call to action is imperative and must be followed to establish a new order for ourselves.

The turnip patch gives us more of ourselves than we can imagine. What we have tossed out or ignored may well be influencing us; what we have chosen to embrace may blind us to its shortcomings. But dig in the darkness we must, in order to move on to further engagement with our wolf.

The next day, the wolf returned again to the pig's house. In a calm voice he spoke to the pig through the door, "Little pig, Farmer Brown has an orchard with scrumptious apples. This is the perfect time in the season for them; they are falling from the trees, just waiting for us to pick them up. Would you like to come with me?"

The pig said, "Of course. What time shall we leave?"

The wolf replied, "Five o'clock," and bid the pig good day.

The little pig, thinking he would redo the trick from the turnip patch, went to the orchard an hour early. But it was much further away than he had anticipated.

While he was in a tree picking apples, he saw the wolf loping up the path, coming in his direction. To his horror, the wolf padded right to the bottom of the tree in which he stood. The wolf drooled in anticipation in spite of himself. Absently licking his chops, he asked, "Are the apples ripe for picking?"

The pig stammered, "Y-y-yes, they taste wonderful, too. Here, you must have one."

The pig hurled the apple as far as he could throw it. The sweet, red, juicy fruit rolled down the hill, and the wolf chased it as if he was pulled by an invisible thread of greed.

Taking advantage of this opportunity, the pig jumped down from the tree and scurried home as fast as his chubby little legs could carry him, clutching his prized basket of apples tightly to his side. He fell into his house and quickly bolted the door against the hunger of the wolf.

The Apple Orchard

Way to go pig! Once again he bested the wolf and is secure. Using his knowledge of the wolf's behavior, he narrowly saved himself by the hair of his chinny, chin, chin.

First, in the turnip patch, the pig learned from his "wolf self." He accomplished this by digging the turnips—uncovering that which had been buried in the darkness—and finding some useful behaviors there. Through the use of experiments, the pig was able to absorb this "wolf knowledge" and apply it to the wolf himself.

In the apple orchard the little pig had his first face-to-face encounter with the wolf. He didn't plan to confront the wolf directly. In fact, it had been his hope to avoid direct confrontation altogether by the same trick he had used before. The trick had lost its effectiveness, but the pig understood it too late. In a split second the pig realized his worst nightmare was taking place. He came eye to eye with the wolf. Now he was forced to face the fear he had been avoiding. He had to face his own dark side, or else his life would be consumed trying to deny its existence. All this was necessary in the scheme of personal development. From direct confrontation with his worst nightmare, the pig would become competent to face his new future.

The Worst Nightmare

What is your worst nightmare? What are the things you find yourself denying or avoiding at all costs? What do you fear more than anything else? Success? Telling yourself the truth? The repetition of your past? Being promiscuous? Becoming responsible for yourself? Being abandoned? Intimacy? Being told what to do? Becoming healthy? Being dependent on someone else? The worst nightmare is not the worst thing that can happen, like the death of someone close to you; it is an encounter with the part of yourself that you refuse to see.

At the apple orchard phase of development our worst nightmare will come loping down the path towards us, demanding to be dealt with. We must stay in contact with it long enough to see the next step. Looking through the lens of our denial, our worst nightmare is obscured. In the initial face to face confrontation, we see only our fears. At this point, we typically run back into old patterns for safety, oblivious to the fact that we are not safe, but living in denial.

This reminds me of a woman who chose the safety of denial over growth. She did not think much of herself. Her appearance was unkempt and her environment in disarray. She behaved in a scattered, frantic manner that spilled into her professional life. Growing up fearing her own beauty and dynamism, her sensuality and full womanhood became her deep shadow. Her worst nightmare was that she would become awakened to those qualities and then be overwhelmed by them. Secretly she envied the woman in her shadow and at the same time she despised her. As a result of counseling to save a shaky relationship, she took the risk of allowing herself to become a powerful, sensual, vibrant, successful woman. Soon she found herself right in the middle of her worst nightmare. What did she do? She scurried quickly back into her brick house of defenses by sabotaging her successful business and relationship. She could not tolerate staying in the apple orchard and facing the wolf. Success in this stage of development occurs only when one is willing to stay face to face with the worst nightmare.

From this point on in the story, a more profound level of impeccability is demanded of the pig. The encounter between the pig and the wolf at the apple tree can still end with the pig being consumed. Through his experiments in the turnip patch, he matured to an understanding of the nature of the wolf. Now he must act on this knowledge. Although the pig learned about the wolf's compulsive nature he himself was now free of choiceless compulsion. This is symbolized by his willingness to release his apple and throw it to the wolf as an offering. When the pig tossed the apple, he knew that the wolf would be pulled by his greed down the hill.

Greed

The compulsive greed of the wolf shows up in all positions of power. Religious and political leaders, for example, arrive at the apple orchard stage of development with its fruits of power not fully realizing the import of their circumstance. Attaining this power is actually a process initiation because it happens over time and has the potential to push one across the boundary into greatness.

In the apple orchard, the leaders' every wish is treated as a demand. Fascinated by what surrounds them, they pluck and eat the fruits at will. If they stay in the orchard too long their greed overtakes them. They use the fruits solely for themselves, forgetting the greater needs of their flocks and constituents. Eventually they feel guilt or shame and, in an attempt to escape it, they deny it. Their very denial creates the wolf as the missing opposite they refuse to claim. Again the wolf is made the designated evil one. Thus, by their very denial, they have summoned the wolf into the orchard because they are there and he is their own self. With unerring accuracy, they eventually bring about their own demise.

In our own ways, we are all subject to the same dilemma. Very clearly, temptation is part of growth; it determines whether or not we are qualified for our next step. We must pass through the orchard without getting caught by greed. If not, we will either spiral down into earlier stages of growth, or move in monotonous circles until we learn the lesson of the orchard: power exists for service. Only then, with our basket of powers firmly in hand, can we walk out of the orchard whole.

Spiritual Awareness

Here the story takes a turn into even deeper meaning: the pig's nature changes, the quest changes, and the role of the wolf changes. The wolf taught the pig his lessons well. The pig absorbed his mentor in the turnip patch, and demonstrated his understanding in the apple orchard. Now the pig's quest becomes more purely spiritual, guiding him towards deeper mysteries. The wolf, aware that he has a qualified student before him, becomes the great teacher—Merlin, guru, the shaman initiator, the profound guide who illuminates the darkness.

The pig is finally beginning to understand what's happening to him, and the significance of life is becoming clear. The relationship between the psyche and the small light of self-awareness deepens: wolves eat pigs. The pig's spiritual learning then dawns: he must change this situation!

Human development unfolds as the emergence of self-awareness and conscious volition out of a pattern of instinctual drives. As a result of escaping from the symbiotic relationship called instinct, we have a constant buried fear of being pulled back in, swallowed up in the vast sea of unconsciousness. Ritual acts are performed to create a sense of safety from this fear of being consumed: animals are sacrificed to the gods, humans and their substitutes (fruit, unleavened bread, incense) are offered, old men send young men to war.

Substitute Sacrifice

Substitute sacrifice, in which one object is sacrificed in exchange for another, is a motif common in our myth and, thus, our politics. Persephone gave Psyche a task requiring her to venture into the underworld. In order to gain safe passport, Psyche tossed a substitute offering of bread to the three headed hound, Cerberus. More commonplace was the upper class practice of paying for a substitute to take their place in battle. This occurred from ancient times through the American civil war, and even beyond. Substitute sacrifices[*] are used psychologically in the hope of forestalling annihilation by the forces in the darkness.

The most feared force of all, death, drives most sacrificial offerings. Death is the ultimate triumph of primordial unconsciousness over the emerged self-awareness. Life is full of expiatory sacrifices to ward off this inevitable outcome and its foretastes. (Dear God, if you let me pass this test, I'll be good.) When offerings are made, the unconscious appears to be temporarily appeased.

In the apple tree, the pig is performing just such a ritual. In addition, he readies himself to join the rank of those who defeat death. While the pig offers a substitute sacrifice (the apple) as a ritual of appeasement, he also consciously lays claim to his wholeness. He realizes that he no longer needs anyone to be the intermediary between

---

* Ken Wilber, *The Atman Project.* 1980, Quest, p. 106. Also Raymond Schwager, S.J., *Must There Be Scapegoats?* 1987, Harper and Row, p. 46, 47.

himself and his psyche. The pig has made his own sacrifice, thereby claiming direct connection to his spirituality. He is his own priest.

The pig has entered the orchard, its trees heavy with ripe fruit. He has the proffered apple in his grasp, but rather than eat it, he tosses it down the hill as an offering for the wolf. In releasing the fruit, the pig makes a sacrifice to substitute for himself. In appropriate primal fashion, the wolf follows the offering down the hill. The pig will later come to realize the even greater significance of this act, namely, the one who eats the apple is the one who gets eaten.

The pig has achieved three great powers in his initiatory experience in the tree. First, he has come to understand the nature of the wolf to the point where he can direct the wolf's behavior. Second, by operating consciously in the mysterious workings of the psyche, the pig has claimed for himself the power that has been ceded to the priestly caste throughout history—the appeasement of the gods. Third, the pig has consciously assumed the primordial power of the ritual; he is awake to the nature of life. He runs home with a basket full of new power symbolized by the remaining apples. The pig has become the great seeker competent to know great truths.

Safe at home again, the little pig waited. Predictably, the wolf was soon knocking at his door.

"My dear little pig," said the wolf, for by now he had grown quite fond of the pig and had begun to respect him through their encounters, "there is a fair taking place in the nearby town. I would like to accompany you there. Seeing that we have so much in common, I am confident that we would find our travels and companionship most rewarding. Shall we meet here at four o'clock tomorrow morning and go to the fair together?"

The pig said, "Fine, that would be delightful," and prepared himself for the next day's journey to the fair, planning as usual to leave his house an hour early.

The sun was not yet peeking over the horizon when the pig stole away for the fair. The wolf, however, had no intention of going. He sat at home, laying plans for the pig's return.

The Fair

What is that wolf up to? The paradox of his role as teacher and devourer is indeed rich.

The pig's awakening at the orchard told the wolf that he was ready to go to the fair. The fair represents the larger world full of new ideas, rich spiritual experiences, profound teachings, deep philosophies. The teacher sends the student to this wealthy environment to deepen his maturity. Because the pig has acquired knowledge, wisdom, and skills through his paradoxical relationship with the teacher, he must now go off into the world to penetrate the innermost depths of life.

The pig departs from his teacher as he departed from his mother and the brick house of safety. This time, however, he is awake to his purpose in life. He is empowered within his own selfhood, and committed to the call of a conscious future that stands on the shoulders of his past. This departure signifies another initiation for the pig—a departure from the now-familiar interaction with the teacher into a new unknown. The pig will leave the wolf only temporarily; once he has explored the fair, he will return to his teacher for further steps in his development.

The fair displays all the powers of mind for the qualified seeker. The pig has acquired the right to know them through his previous interaction with his teacher and by claiming his self. He has awakened the resources to make even deeper sense of the mystery of life. Equipped with a richer self that he discovered and matured in antagonistic cooperation with the wolf, he is sent into the wealthy learning environment of the fair by the master to return as a qualified partner.

Teachers and Teachings

There is a commandment in the Judeo-Christian scriptures that says, "Thou shalt not steal." One interpretation of this prescription is germane to our story: "Thou canst not steal." If we do not have the capacity to absorb a level of growth, it will slip through our fingers like sand clutched too tightly, or it will eat us up like the wolf ate the first two pigs. We cannot keep what we are incapable of holding. If someone gets a million dollars, he had better hurry up and become a millionaire so he will get to keep the money. Unless he does, the million dollars will go by the same route that his other money has gone. An ancient teaching says that a fool who falls asleep in front of a sage will still wake up a fool.

Many levels of teaching are essential for our development, even though they may be difficult or convoluted. In traveling through this maze, a teacher is necessary, especially for the deeper dimensions of growth. Life provides us with teachers until we are wise enough to find our own—an embodiment of the true master. All are wolves; all are committed to our awakening; all show us our darkness and lead us to a glimmer of our hidden light.

Each pig evolved a different level of teaching out of his own interaction with life. From being consumed by their failures, to being possessed by cultural edicts, to finally having the darkness become explicit and externalized in the embodiment of another, the pigs were taught.

We can say that each of the pigs' learnings, as well as each of these darknesses, expresses itself as the wolf.

- The voracious devourer who stands guard at the gate is the other side of our frivolous immaturity.
- The wolf who eats up the rigidity of our unexamined life is the other side of our naivete.
- The wolf who challenges the validity of our defenses is the other side of our arrogance.
- The wolf who invites us to mine our darkness is the expression of all we reject in ourselves.
- The wolf who is our worst nightmare is the expression of our fear of ourselves.
- The wolf who chases the apple down the hill is the expression of our greed and compulsion.
- The wolf who sends us off to the fair is the embodiment of our commitment to learn.

All of these wolves are life pushing us into more life.

Maturing to the point of having a competent embodied teacher is a step of great proportion. One who has already mastered the student's current developmental stage will serve as the essential correcting mechanism to challenge the student's confusion, limits and arrogance.

As we saw, the wolf never intended to accompany the pig to the fair because a proper teacher makes the student independent. A teacher of this caliber is rare in the world; rarer still is a fully qualified student. First the teacher examines the student from afar to see if he or she is qualified. The important second step is the examination of the teacher by the student. This examination must prove the teacher selfless. Once the testing has been settled to the satisfaction of both, the student lets go of testing and starts to learn.

In life, our wolf nature repeatedly works with our pig nature in the first and second pig stages until finally we look within at our own dark side. We're no longer driven to project it outside as the wolf. The pig nature, gaining sanctuary from its naivete in the third pig stage, begins to take the charge of life away from the benign care of myth, culture, and naive actions of self-preservation and claim that responsibility for itself. At this point we also formally choose a teacher and, therefore, a philosophy, just like the pig did prior to going to the fair.

Choosing a Philosophy

A philosophy of life will serve to organize our method of inquiry. As we move through the various stages of our pig nature, we will come into contact with many teachers and their philosophies. A variety of teachings makes valuable contributions but, at some point, we will find that we resonate to one. Eventually it will become important to have one teacher and philosophy so we can resolve the conflicts of method between teachers and teaching styles that will arise. The methods are many; the truth is one.

It is a rare system of thinking that can tolerate critique. Some philosophies can take a seeker only so far, and some seekers can advance only so far. It is apparent, then, that critique of philosophy as well as of seeker is an essential self-correcting mechanism. When naming the profound experiences that occur in deeper self-unfoldment, most philosophies wrap their seekers in a strict belief system. By virtue of what they include, they exclude everything else, especially some vital realizations. Periodically revising our philosophy of life as we live it is, therefore, a critically valuable exercise.

A unique bond has been established between the pig and the wolf. Much has taken place between them that could only happen in the teacher/student relationship. The pig, entering deeper into the complexity of life, will now temper his experience with the knowledge he gained from the wolf. Let us see how he will make the wolf's knowledge his own.

The little pig was quite late in returning home from the fair. He purchased a butterchurn there and was carrying it back with him. Pleased with his purchase, he smiled to himself as he strode purposefully along.

Keeping his eyes open for the wolf, the pig neared his residence. He stopped on the hilltop above his house and spied the wolf leaning against the tree in his very yard!

The Butterchurn

The butterchurn in the possession of the pig is like the trophy that the triumphant seeker brings back from his quest. In many myths the hero or heroine returns with a trophy that represents the accomplishments of their quest as well as their victory over the forces that beset them. In the *Kathopanishada,* Nachiketa endured his contest with Yama, the King of Death, and returned with a many-colored chain, symbolizing his knowledge of the secret of death. Cinderella likewise endured many trials before dancing at the ball and receiving the glass slipper, a sign of her integration. So our little pig, having endured several interactions with the wolf, and after learning many things at the fair, returns with the butterchurn.

The butterchurn symbolizes the much-prized faculty of discrimination. Deemed of utmost importance in many spiritual traditions, discrimination is the ability to make boundaries, to see them clearly, and use them to serve us. A churn "discriminates," or separates, butter, cream, and whey—all present in the common substance of milk. It makes many products out of one by the motion of a central shaft and paddle. In addition to being a metaphor for making distinctions in life, the churn is a metaphor for the organization of human experience.

Ancient Eastern philosophies have a matching metaphor in the chakra system. It is a model which charts the various stages of human development through discrimination. The word *chakra* means "turning wheel." Like the paddle of the butterchurn separating milk, it separates the substance of mind into the basic human behaviors of security, sexuality, power, unconditional love, compassion, and intuition.

The central shaft and paddle of his churn represent the pig's ability to animate and create distinctions himself. He now has the knowledge to form many out of the one, to consciously take potential and make it actual. By bringing home a butterchurn, the pig demonstrates that he has the power of his chakra system in hand. With this power, the pig returns to his teacher. He is at the threshold of the next major turning point in his quest.

What should the pig do? The wolf sat between the door to his house and himself. Thinking quickly, the pig crawled inside the butterchurn and rolled with it down the hill. Faster and faster he went, right up to the startled wolf, who ran out of his path as fast as he could run.

The pig landed at his door, climbed out of the churn, and went inside the house. Quite pleased with himself, he drew the bolt against the wolf one final time.

Face to Face Confrontation

At the foot of the hill, the teacher waited to find out if the student had acquired the right for the final initiation. The wolf knows that the final confrontation is at hand. His student passed the initiations of the brick house, the turnips, the apples, and now the butterchurn. The pig must make use of these resources to take on the final quest—the master himself.

The Zen master, Sokei-an, spoke of the necessity of a strong student in order to ensure that the *dharma* (teachings) be passed on. "When a Zen teacher transmits his *dharma* it is a championship fight. The disciple must knock him down, show him his attainment, knowledge and new information. Zen still exists because of this iron rule. Before the female hawk will copulate with the male she flies for three days through the sky with the male pursuing her; only one who can overtake her can have her. The Zen master is like the female hawk, and the disciple is like the male. You must not forget this law."*

This point was demonstrated in the television series, *Kung Fu*. Kane, a young neophyte in a Buddhist monastery, was invited to pluck a proffered stone from his master's hand. When Kane tried to do this, the master quickly closed his fingers over the stone and replied, "When you are able to take this stone from my hand, it will be time for you to leave."

Throughout their relationship, the pig has desperately tried to avoid contact with the wolf. The initiation of contact has always been left to the wolf, making him the carrier of the pig's denied aggression. This time the pig has definitely initiated contact. We can say that the butterchurn encounter serves as the antidote to the pig's avoidance and denial of aggression.

In taking the offensive, the pig climbed inside the butterchurn, showing that he has become the embodiment of everything he has learned. The butterchurn itself becomes a crucible in which the base substance of the pig's awareness is transformed into gold.

* Anne Bancroft. *Zen: Direct Pointing to Reality.* 1979, Crossroad, p. 12.

There is an old alchemic saying, "It is the crucible, not the fire, that makes the gold." Long ago, when the pig left the brick house to go into the turnip patch, it was as if he made the commitment to stay in the arena of transformation with the master, no matter what. His act of climbing into the churn showed his realization of that commitment. Climbing in the crucible is an act of surrender to transformation, an act of strength, not an act of submission. The pig consciously identifies himself with the power of the teachings; with this power he faces the master, who is also the fire of initiation. Their contact is destined to produce the gold of the pig's total integration.

Not to be thwarted, the wolf picked himself up from the ground, dusted himself off, and continued his relentless pursuit of the pig. Looking for an opening, he climbed atop the house, arranging himself to descend through the chimney. He set his jaw and said to himself, "This day someone will be eaten!"

Inside the house, the pig had set a large pot of soup to cook upon the hearth. Smoke from the fire mixed with steam from the boiling vegetables and rose up the smoke stack.

Suddenly there was a loud splash as the wolf descended the chimney and landed in the pot. The startled little pig quickly fastened the pot lid in place so the wolf could not escape.

Final Confrontation

This is a very determined wolf. While sitting on the roof, he resolves his next step. As master teacher, he determines to bring about the fulfillment of the last stage of the pig's quest—assimilation of the master's truth. At this point of development in the story (and in life) there is no turning back for either wolf or pig. The wolf, being wise and committed, knows that the day must end with the death of one of them. His responsibility as teacher must bring it about.

The relationship between the pig and the wolf is one of mutual interdependence. They need each other in order to create a unified whole: the light and the dark. Both must be impeccable in their tasks. The wolf must be an impeccable teacher to mentor the pig into final assimilation; the pig must be an impeccable student to deliberately stand in the face of the master, in the face of the gods. Others have found that feat virtually impossible. Many have sought to avoid it, looking to religion to mediate on their behalf and render the divine harmless.

If the pig does not succeed in his final initiation, he is bound to be consumed by a prior state. At this stage of his development, that in itself would be a death. His imperative is to win or die, to assimilate or be assimilated. Success is his only option.

The motif of encounter to the death is portrayed often in myth and fairy tale. Ulysses must kill the Cyclops or be killed; Jack must slay the giant and escape down the beanstalk or be eaten by the giant; the miller's daughter must destroy Rumplestiltskin by saying his name or suffer the death of her baby daughter. The final imperative against the darkness is not chosen; it is thrust upon one and there is no escape.

In accord with the ancient motif, the wolf pursues the pig to his house, and finding no other entrance, decides to descend into the house through the chimney. This pursuit and descent is replete with rich symbolism.

The descent of the wolf down the chimney portrays the descent of high initiation conferred upon the head of the prepared seeker. The gods have always waited to receive the smoke of the sacrificial offerings made to them by the faithful ones. They wait no more; the gods themselves now descend through the sacred smoke. They descend through the awakened mind of the pig, a mind made strong through contact with his own projections and the projections of the collective. The gods descend to bring the final goal to the faithful pig.

The wolf, likewise, has always waited outdoors for the pig, accepting what the pig would offer. This time, the wolf also waits no more. The wolf now is the embodiment of the pig's initiation. He embodies the descent of grace. He seeks victory for the pig, but knows that the pig must claim it for himself. The pig has become everything the wolf hoped he would be. He followed all the steps of development, and is now on the brink of becoming one of the chosen. Thus he must be pursued.

All the elements for sacrifice are ready: the hearthstone and the cooking vessel are composed of the earth; the soup contains water; the flames are the sacrificial fire; the smoke rides the air; the sky embraces space. As the master which the pig emulates, the wolf descends from the sky, through the smoke, and lands in the earth-hewn crucible that holds the pig's boiling soup.

That evening for supper, the pig ate the wolf.

Integration

The pig does the unthinkable: he eats the wolf. In ordinary reality, wolves eat pigs, neither pigs nor wolves being able to hold the opposite idea in their minds. But this is a new realm of consciousness, one that brings the pig into contact with life in a radically different way. His mere existence now catapults him into a whole new order where he will participate in an entirely new realm of action. The pig is a transformed being.

When the little pig consciously assimilates the wolf, he also assimilates the wolf's knowledge and power. Like Siegfried, who slew the dragon and sucked its vanquished blood from his fingers, like the hunter who eats the still-warm heart of his kill, and even like the child who consumes the mother at her breast, the pig eats the wolf, taking power and nurturance. Religious rituals likewise enact the eating of the body of their redeemers in order to acquire spiritual power and grace.

When he eats the wolf, the pig assimilates his own demons as well as his nurturer. He becomes a mystic, raised above the rest of the community, because like the mystic, he has embraced the wolf. Mystics descend into the underworld in their quest, emerging with themselves as the trophy. They have awakened to their deeper self, and now are able to embody the full truth—the light and the dark, the mortal and the immortal, the alpha of innocence and the omega of maturity.

Our story ends with the pig returning into life with a unique sense of wholeness. Awakened now, and with his shadow integrated, he has transcended some measure of the unconscious collective and individual self. This task has been an extraordinary accomplishment. Because of it the pig has claimed the right to engage the next unknowns in a succession of further unknowns.

The relationship of pigs and wolves is not a battle. It is the unconditioned desire to know truth. It is the willingness to periodically re-examine truth. It is the courage to face your own darkness and the wisdom to let it partner you into divinity.

Afterword

The Wolf as Teacher

This is an amazing little book. Charles Bates has taken The Three Little Pigs story and has pulled an immense amount of useful information and even knowledge out of it. I knew the story only in its shorter version, and it tugged at my mind from time to time, but I never studied it. Charles did, and I admire three points in his celebration and interpretation of the story.

The first is his discussion of "second-pig thinking." We all associate the straw and the sticks and the bricks with ways of protection or styles of building, but he associates those three substances with ways of thinking. "Second-pig thinking" amounts to using the same principles in our new project that have clearly failed in earlier projects. We can do that in private life and also in national life. Intervention failed when we tried it in Vietnam, and so we try it again in Iraq. The government's thought in this manner is clearly "second-pig thinking." "Third-pig thinking" means a radical shift, a kind of leap, trying something no pigs have tried before, and that shift depends on a clearer grasp of the wolf.

The wolf in this book stands for the shadow side of each of us—those dark, greedy, cunning, base, untrustworthy, unacceptable traits. We usually split them off from ourselves and assign them to another person or another country. I remember once asking an experienced old therapist at a lecture how an ordinary person, let's say a 40-year-old woman in a small town, could begin to do some shadow work. He said she can't unless she knows the concept of the shadow. That seemed harsh to all of us, and so he added, "There's one more

91

way; if there is some other person in that town whom she absolutely hates, and if she could break eye contact, so to speak, with that person and quickly look down to her left, she would see her own shadow." That's very good. And we know that if there's anything the pig hates, it's the wolf. Following Charles Bates' interpretation of the story, then, the wolf is the shadow of the sweet little pig.

In "third-pig thinking," each of us has to have close contact with the wolf. Bates says, "The wolf has behaviors that he uses to be successful; the pig now claims some of them for himself." For example, the third pig tricks the wolf by arriving at the turnip patch one hour early in the morning. Turnip digging is associated with rooting out what is dark and hidden in ourselves, and Bates remarks, " . . . the pig realizes that he and the wolf are inextricably linked. Their strong attraction comes from a bond deep in their psyches." We could say that the closer each of us comes to our maturity, the stronger the attraction of the wolf to us. This idea is a very powerful rebuke to fundamentalist thinking whether in church circles or in government circles. If Russia for thirty years has been our wolf, then the two of us must have a bond deep in the psyche, and we need more close contact. That, in fact, is exactly what Robert Frost urged when he visited Khrushchev during the Cold War. He told Khrushchev that America and Russia should set up a cultural competition with each other and see who could be best in poetry, in painting, in exploration of space, in philosophy, and so on. In our personal lives when we begin to feel a strong attraction to people we've always hated, we know that we are beginning to work on our dark side.

A third thing I like about Bates' discussion is his unfolding of apparently innocent details. For example, when the wolf comes upon the pig in the apple orchard and the pig finds himself insecurely hidden in the apple tree, he throws a fine red apple as far as he can down the hill. " . . . and the wolf chased it as if he was pulled by an invisible thread of greed." Bates suggests that the apple belongs to the whole world of sacrifice. Some sacrifices are done to distract the dark forces so one can get home. When the pig later visits the fair, the wolf tries to catch him by going to the pig's house and waiting there for the pig to come back. It turns out that the pig has bought or earned a butterchurn at the fair. Milk contains butter, cream, and whey, all mingled together, and the churn was invented to separate and discriminate between them. The story says that only after the hero's contact with the wolf does he learn to discriminate, to separate the spiritual "butter" from the rest of the milk. The Persian poet, Rumi, writing about 1245 A.D. says:

> Butter is hidden inside buttermilk . . .
> For a thousand years all people see is buttermilk.
> The butter has disappeared; no one knows where it is.
> At last God sends a churner. He twists the big wooden stick
> cunningly, he teaches me where my inner one is.
> This milk has been around a long time.
> Don't stop working with it until the butter appears.
>   (Version by R.B.)

Charles Bates unfolds a charming detail in this scene of the pig and the churner. When the pig, returning from the fair, arrives on a hill above his house and sees the wolf waiting, he gets inside the butterchurn and rolls himself down the hill. In this way he frightens the wolf from his post at the door. This is a wonderful idea—how the butterchurn helps in the struggle with the dark side.

As the story closes, it becomes clear that the more one works with the dark side, the more it becomes a teacher. Bates' last brilliant stroke in this discussion is to point out that the story ends with the pig's eating the wolf just as a good student eats his teacher. Winston Churchill said, "I've often had to eat my own words, and I found the diet very nourishing." So each of us, when we leave "second-pig thinking" with its endless repetition of old mistakes, can find a way to regard our enemy as a teacher, bring him closer in a shrewd way, and finally nourish ourselves by eating all those parts of us that in the first half of our life we threw away.

Robert Bly

Bibliography

Ashliman, D. L. *A Guide to Folktales in the English Language*. (New York: Greenwood Press, 1987)

Barfield, Owen. *Saving the Appearances: A Study in Idolatry*. (New York: Harcourt, Brace & World).

Bellah, Robert, et al. *Habits of the Heart: Individualism and Commitment in American Life*. (Berkeley: University of California Press, 1985).

Bharati, Agehananda. *The Light at the Center: Context and Pretext of Modern Mysticism*. (Santa Barbara: Ross-Erickson, 1976).

Bly, Robert. *Iron John: A Book About Men*. (Reading, MA: Addison-Wesley, 1990).

Bly, Robert, ed. William Booth. *A Little Book on the Human Shadow. New York: Harper and Row, 1988)*.

Campbell, Joseph. *The Hero with a Thousand Faces*. (Princeton: Princeton University Press, 1973).

Campbell, Joseph. *The Inner Reaches of Outer Space: Metaphor as Myth and as Religion*. (New York: Alfred Van der Mark, 1986).

Daly, Robert. *Must There be Scapegoats?: Violence and Redemption in the Bible*. (San Francisco: Harper and Row, 1978).

DeMott, Benjamin. *The Imperial Middle: Why Americans Can't Think Straight About Class*. (New York: William Morrow and Company, 1990).

Eisler, Raine. *The Chalice and the Blade: Our History, Our Future*. (San Francisco, Harper and Row, 1987).

Farrell, Warren. *Why Men Are the Way They Are*. (New York: McGraw Hill, 1986).

Gardner, Howard. *Frames of Mind: The Theory of Multiple Intelligences.* (New York: Basic Books, Inc., 1985).

Gilligan, Carol. *In A Different Voice: Psychological Theory and Women's Development.* (Cambridge, MA: Harvard University Press, 1982).

Goleman, Daniel. *Vital Lies, Simple Truths: The Psychology of Self Deception.* (New York: Simon and Schuster, Inc., 1985).

Hagberg, Janet. *Real Power: Stages of Personal Power in Organizations.* (Minneapolis: Winston Press, 1984).

Hall, Edward T. *Beyond Culture.* (New York: Doubleday and Co., 1976).

Handy, Charles. *The Age of Unreason.* (London: Business Books, Ltd., 1989).

Jacobs, Joseph. *English Fairy Tales.* (New York: G. P. Putnam, 1987).

Keen, Sam. *Faces of the Enemy: Reflections of the Hostile Imagination.* (San Francisco: Harper and Row, 1986).

Lederer, Wolfgang. *The Fear of Women.* (New York: Harcourt, Brace, Jovanovich, 1968).

Maslow, Abraham. *Toward a Psychology of Being.* (New York: Van Nostrand Reinhold Company, 1968).

Miller, Alice. *For Your Own Good: Hidden Cruelty in Child Rearing and the Roots of Violence.* (New York: Farrah, Straus, Giroux, 1983).

Nodding, Nel. *Women and Evil.* (Berkeley, CA: University of California Pres, 1989).

O'Brien, Justin. *The Wellness Tree: Energizing Yourself in Body, Mind and Spirit.* (St. Paul, MN: Yes International, 1990).

O'Brien, Theresa King. *The Spiral Path: Essays and Interviews in Women's Spirituality.* (St. Paul, MN: Yes International Publishers, 1988).

Pagels, Elaine. *Adam, Eve and the Serpent.* (New York: Random House, 1988).

Pearce, Joseph Chilton. *Magical Child Matures.* (New York: E. P. Dutton, 1985).

Peck, M. Scott. *People of the Lie: The Hope for Healing Human Evil.* (New York: Simon and Schuster, 1983).

Perera, Sylvia Brinton. *The Scapegoat Complex: Toward a Mythology of Shadow and Guilt.* (Toronto: Inner City Books, 1986).

Perls, Fritz. *Ego, Hunger and Aggression.* (New York: Random House, 1969).

Reed, Evelyn. *Woman's Evolution: From Matriarchal Clan to Patriarchal Family.* (New York: Pathfinder Press, 1975).

Schaef, Anne Wilson. *When Society Becomes an Addict.* (San Francisco: Harper and Row, 1987).

Schmookler, Andrew Bard. *Out of Weakness: Healing the Wounds that Drive Us to War.* (Toronto: Bantam Books, 1988).

Tiger, Lionel. *Men in Groups.* (New York: Marion Boyars, 1984).

Tillman, James A. *Why America Needs Racism and Poverty.* (Four Winds Press, 1969).

Von Franz, Marie. *Individuation in Fairy Tales.* (Zurich: Spring Publications, 1977).

Von Franz, Marie. *Shadow and Evil in Fairy Tales.* (Dallas: Spring Publications, 1974).

Weatherford, Jack. *Indian Givers: How Indians of the Americas Transformed the World.* (New York: Fawcett Columbine, 1988).

Wilber, Ken. *Eye to Eye: The Quest for the New Paradigm.* (Garden City, NY: Anchor Press, Doubleday, 1983).

Wilber, Ken. *Up from Eden: A Transpersonal View of Human Evolution.* (Boulder, CO: Shambhala, 1983).

Zimmer, Heinrich. *The King and the Corpse: Tales of the Soul's Quest of Evil.* (Princeton: Princeton University Press, 1957).

About the Author

Charles Bates is a nationally known consultant and lecturer in the fields of organizational development, leadership, cultural diversity, stress management, and holistic personal development. He is also a noted exponent of hatha yoga and mind-body integration. He is a member of NTL (National Training Laboratories), a consultant with the Gestalt Institute of Cleveland, and adjunct faculty of The College of St. Catherine, St. Paul, where he team-teaches a graduate course in Leadership and Spirituality.

His concentration on mind-body interconnections and its application to the chemical dependency field led to his first book, *Ransoming the Mind: An Integration of Yoga and Modern Therapy.* He has also co-authored *Mirrors for Men,* and is a columnist for *Insight* newspaper of Minneapolis/St. Paul.

Bates has been a student of mysticism for over twenty-two years, studying in India, Nepal, Japan, and the U.S., and conducts retreats and workshops nationally on leadership, relationships, personal development and spirituality.